THE MUMMY'S CURSE

BY LISA OWINGS

EPIC

BELLWETHER MEDIA · MINNEAPOLIS, MN

EPIC BOOKS are no ordinary books. They burst with intense action, high-speed heroics, and shadows of the unknown. Are you ready for an Epic adventure?

This edition first published in 2015 by Bellwether Media, Inc.

No part of this publication may be reproduced in whole or in part without written permission of the publisher. For information regarding permission, write to Bellwether Media, Inc., Attention: Permissions Department, 5357 Penn Avenue South, Minneapolis, MN 55419.

Library of Congress Cataloging-in-Publication Data

Owings, Lisa.
   The Mummy's Curse / by Lisa Owings.
      pages cm. – (Epic. Unexplained Mysteries)
   Includes bibliographical references and index.
   Summary: "Engaging images accompany information about the mummy's curse. The combination of high-interest subject matter and light text is intended for students in grades 2 through 7"– Provided by publisher.
   Audience: Ages 7-12.
   ISBN 978-1-62617-203-6 (hardcover : alk. paper)
   1. Mummies–Juvenile literature. I. Title.
   GN293.O85 2015
   393'.3–dc23
                                2014039981

Designed by Jon Eppard.

Printed in the United States of America, North Mankato, MN.

TABLE OF CONTENTS

DO NOT DISTURB

Two researchers enter a **tomb** in Egypt. Their lamps bob over piles of **rubble**. In a dark corner, something catches the light. It is a chest with a golden latch.

They open the dusty chest. Inside is a **scroll** covered in writing. "Do not **disturb** this tomb!" it warns. Days later, one of the researchers falls ill. Could they have been **cursed**?

TALES FROM THE TOMB

The mummy's curse is a **legend**. Stories say anyone who disturbs a mummy's rest will suffer. They may have a little bad luck. Or they may be **doomed** to die.

A TITANIC CURSE?

Some claim a mummy was aboard the *Titanic*. They say the mummy's curse caused the great ship to sink.

Howard Carter

This legend may have begun long ago in Egypt. But it became widely known in 1922. Researcher Howard Carter found King Tutankhamen's tomb that year.

THE FIRST WARNING

Stories say Carter brought a canary with him to Egypt. But the bird was killed by a cobra. Some think this was a warning to stay away.

PALL MALL

GAZETTE AND GLOBE

London's Most Influential Evening Paper.

THURSDAY, APRIL 5, 1923.

No. 18,045.

[REGISTERED AT THE G.P.O. AS A NEWSPAPER]

LORD CARNARVON'S

EXPERTS AND A LUXOR "POISON TRAP."

SUPERSTITIOUS BELIEFS RIDICULED BY WELL-KNOWN EGYPTOLOGISTS.

TRAGEDY OF HIS DEATH.

EARL WHO FOUND TUTANKHAMEN'S TOMB, BUT NEVER SAW THE MUMMY.

The death of Lord Carnarvon, coming swiftly upon the heels of his great triumph—the discovery of the tomb of Pharaoh Tutankhamen in the Valley of the Kings—has created widespread controversy.

There will probably be thousands who see in the Earl's fate the "black arts" of the ancient Egyptians, while on the other hand the theory of a poison trap in the tomb is advanced.

Below, the "Pall Mall Gazette" publishes the views of well-known Egyptologists and pathologists, who ridicule, without exception, the theory that poison was left in the tomb for the purpose of dealing death to intruders.

Lord Carnarvon died peacefully in the early hours of this morning. He was conscious almost to the last.

The tragedy of his death lies in the fact that he never saw the mummy of the Pharaoh he discovered. He had deferred that for a year.

NO THOUGHT OF "VENGEANCE."

EGYPTIANS' PRACTICE TO PROTECT
BY POISONS.

THE NEW LORD AND LADY CAR

A HITHERTO UNPUBLISHED PHOTOGRAPH OF
WHO SUCCEEDS TO THE EARLDOM, A

LORD CARNARVON'S LAST HOURS.

DEATH AFTER HOPES OF RECOVERY.

PEACEFUL END.

BODY TO BE EMBALMED AND BROUGHT HOME.

CAIRO, Thursday.

Lord Carnarvon brightened considerably yesterday afternoon, inspiring the hope that he had beaten the crisis, but towards midnight he began to weaken rapidly, and just before two o'clock he died peacefully.

A London specialist, who was called up the case, did not take up this morning,

CHE

ACTIO

Months later, his research partner Lord Carnarvon died. Others who had entered the tomb died in the following years. The mummy's curse seemed more real than ever.

Howard Carter

Lord Carnarvon

CURSE OR COINCIDENCE?

Believers claim a **tablet** found in the tomb warned of the curse. They say the lights in Cairo went out when Lord Carnarvon died. Some think this was a sign of the curse.

ANOTHER VICTIM?

A man who knew Carter jumped from a building in 1930. A letter he left said he could not stand any more horrors. Was he talking about the curse?

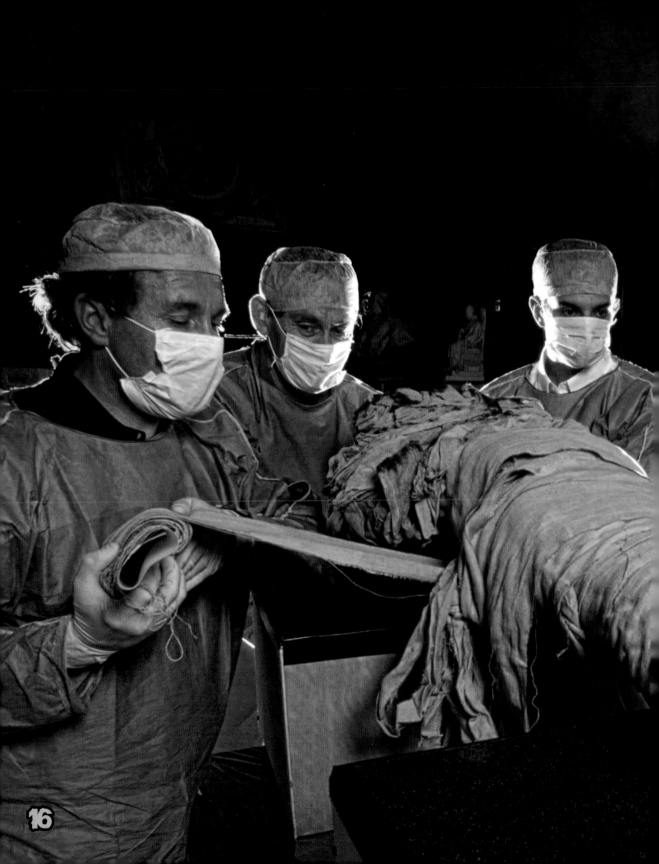

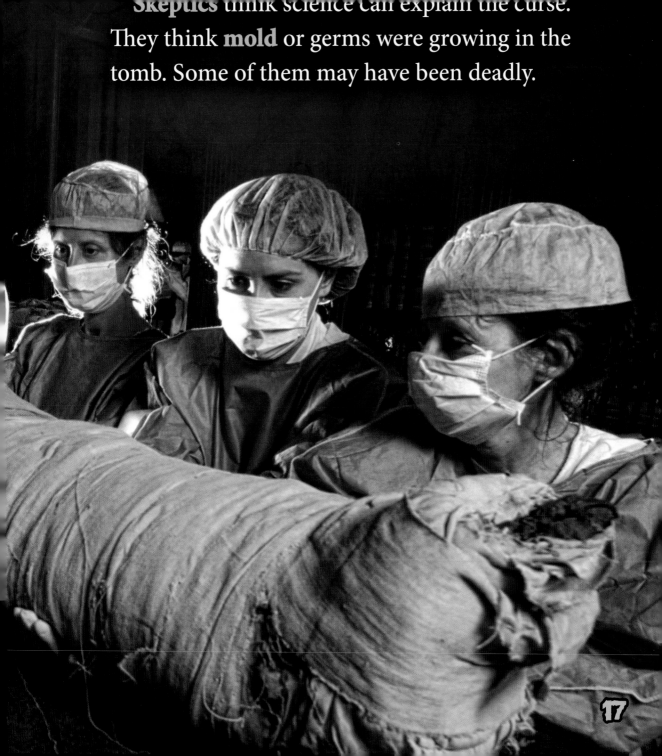

Skeptics think science can explain the curse. They think **mold** or germs were growing in the tomb. Some of them may have been deadly.

Other people say the deaths and other events were by chance. Most people who had entered the tomb lived long, healthy lives. The "curse" simply made a good story.

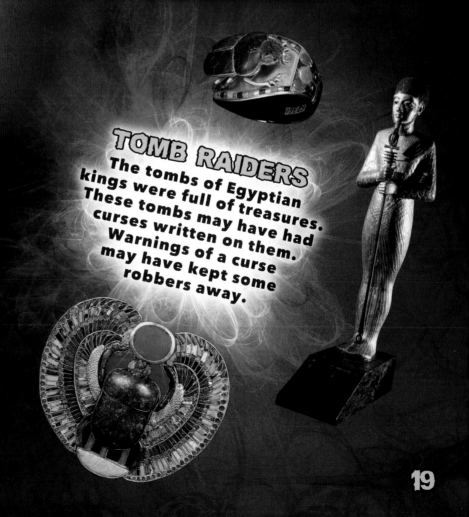

TOMB RAIDERS

The tombs of Egyptian kings were full of treasures. These tombs may have had curses written on them. Warnings of a curse may have kept some robbers away.

KING TUT'S CURSE

LORD CARNARVON
Carter's research partner; entered the tomb
Died of blood poisoning and pneumonia (1923)

SIR BRUCE INGHAM
Carter's friend; given a gift from the tomb
House burned down, then flooded

GEORGE JAY GOULD
Visited the tomb
Died of fever (1923)

AUDREY HERBERT
Lord Carnarvon's half-brother
Went blind; died of blood poisoning (1923)

SIR ARCHIBALD DOUGLAS REID
Examined Tut's mummy
Died of an unknown illness (1924)

RICHARD BETHELL
Carter's secretary; entered the tomb
Died in his sleep (1929)

LORD WESTBURY
Richard Bethell's father
Jumped from building (1930)

No one knows whether the mummy's curse is real. It may have driven many to their deaths. Or it may be just a scary story. Would you disturb a mummy's **eternal** rest?

GLOSSARY

cursed—placed under an evil spell

disturb—to change the way something is arranged, or to bother someone

doomed—unable to escape a terrible event

eternal—lasting forever

legend—a story many people believe that has not been proven true

mold—a kind of fungus that grows in damp areas

rubble—broken pieces of stone left after a structure is destroyed

scroll—a long piece of paper rolled into a tube

skeptics—people who doubt the truth of something

tablet—a piece of stone with writing carved into it

tomb—a grave, room, or building for holding a dead body

TO LEARN MORE

At the Library

Arlon, Penelope. *Ancient Egypt*. New York, N.Y.: Scholastic, 2014.

Carney, Elizabeth. *Mummies*. Washington, D.C.: National Geographic, 2009.

Higgins, Nadia. *Ghosts*. Minneapolis, Minn.: Bellwether Media, 2014.

On the Web

Learning more about the mummy's curse is as easy as 1, 2, 3.

1. Go to www.factsurfer.com.

2. Enter "mummy's curse" into the search box.

3. Click the "Surf" button and you will see a list of related web sites.

With factsurfer.com, finding more information is just a click away.

INDEX